Donated by Dr. Mingshui
Professor of Literacy Educ.
Department of Curriculum & I.

America's
Forests

Guide to Plalants and Animals

Marianne D. Wallace

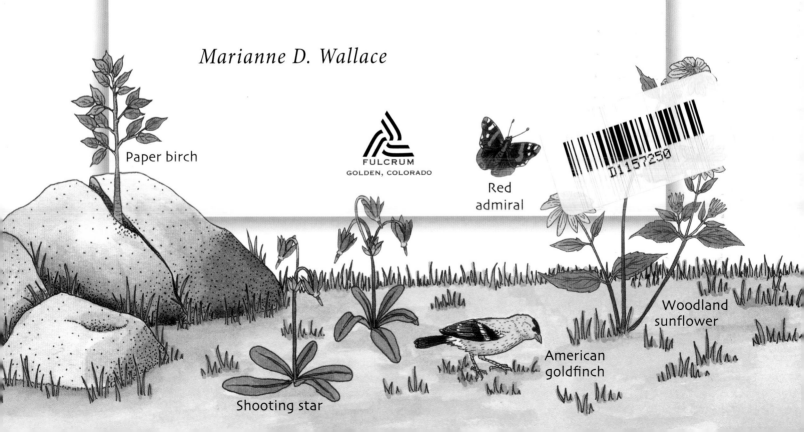

Paper birch

FULCRUM
GOLDEN, COLORADO

Red
admiral

Woodland
sunflower

American
goldfinch

Shooting star

To Grandma Doumakes, who bought the cabin in a forest near Los Angeles where I spent my summers feeding squirrels and climbing trees; to my husband, Gary, who showed me both the misty redwood forests of coastal California where time stops and tree line in the Sierra Nevada where the forests end; and to my friend Trish, who knows all the best hiking trails in the lush, green forests of Great Smoky Mountains National Park.

Plants and animals shown on the front cover (clockwise from upper right): **Scarlet oak, fox squirrel, aspen, white-tailed deer, common blue violets, raccoon, columbine, ruffed grouse, sugar maple, red elderberry, ponderosa pine.**

In title box: **Scarlet oak leaf and blue jay.**

Plants and animals shown on the back cover (clockwise from upper right): **Engelmann Spruce trees, magnolia, red fox, Amanita mushrooms, box turtle, saw palmetto, corn snake, kapok tree, blue morpho butterfly, bromeliad, toucan.**

Text and illustrations copyright © 2009 Marianne D. Wallace

Library of Congress Cataloging-in-Publication Data

Wallace, Marianne D.
   America's forests : guide to plants and animals / Marianne D. Wallace.
      p. cm. -- (America's ecosystems)
   Includes index.
   ISBN 978-1-55591-595-7 (pbk.)
   1. Forests and forestry--North America--Juvenile literature. 2. Forest plants--North America--Juvenile literature. 3. Forest animals--North America--Juvenile literature. 4. Forest ecology--North America--Juvenile literature. I. Title.
   QH102.W345 2009
   578.73097--dc22

            2008041005

Fulcrum Publishing
4690 Table Mountain Drive, Suite 100
Golden, CO 80403
800-992-2908 • 303-277-1623
www.fulcrumbooks.com

Printed in China

0 9 8 7 6 5 4 3 2 1
Design by Ann W. Douden and Patty Maher
Cover image by Marianne D. Wallace

Table of Contents

Paper birch

Chipmunk

Introduction to Forest Life

What is a forest?

To a bird flying high above the treetops, the forest may look like a bumpy carpet in different shades of green. To a squirrel, the forest probably seems like a highway of branches, a place to run from tree to tree. A fox, running on the ground, lives in a forest of shrubs and scattered tree trunks. And down among the leaf litter on the forest floor, the world of a ground beetle is made up of wildflowers, fallen branches, and small patches of bright, spongy moss.

Each layer makes the forest seem different to the different kinds of animals that live there. These layers have names. The area at the top of the trees is called the **canopy** and creates a kind of roof over the forest. Shorter trees beneath the canopy are part of the **understory**. Also in the understory, but usually shorter than most of the trees, is the **shrub layer**. Wildflowers and other small plants are in the **herb layer**. Finally, at the bottom is the **forest floor**.

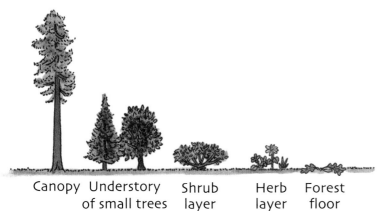

Canopy | Understory of small trees | Shrub layer | Herb layer | Forest floor

Map of Earth

The Earth has over 15 million square miles (almost 4 billion hectares) of forest. That's about 30 percent of the Earth's land surface.

Fallen leaves, along with branches, dead flowers, seeds, fruits, and other plant material that falls to the forest floor are very important to the health of a forest. This **litter** on the ground provides some of the nutrients that the trees and other plants will use in the future. Mushrooms and other fungi help break down, or decompose, much of the litter. And sometimes fires burn the litter and leave ash behind. Either way, the nutrients are washed into the soil, where they can be absorbed by the tree roots. The layer of litter also keeps the forest floor moist and cool and provides hiding places for small animals like salamanders and insects.

Trees grow old and rot, beavers gnaw through tree trunks, and storms move through the forest. In these cases, trees may fall down and leave an opening in the forest canopy. The new sunlit openings, called **forest gaps** or light gaps, create areas where flowers bloom and seeds of sun-loving trees can get started. This is especially important in **closed forests**, where trees grow so close together that very little sunlight can come through and most of the forest floor is shaded.

In drier areas, such as pine forests and savannahs, trees grow farther apart and there is a lot of sunlight on the ground. These are **open forests**. In open forests, fires often keep the vegetation underneath the trees low and prevent most new shrubs and trees from getting started and growing.

Forest trees are usually one of two types: **conifers**, such as pines and hemlocks, that have stiff, needlelike leaves, or **hardwoods**, such as oaks and maples, that have wider, softer, often flat leaves.

Conifers are usually **evergreen**, with leaves that stay on their branches all year long. But many hardwoods are **deciduous**, which means they lose their leaves in the fall. This helps protect the tree from dying during the cold winter. Why? Trees and other plants need liquid water to grow. They draw it up through their roots and use it in their green leaves to make food. But in the

Sugar maple

Aspen

White oak

winter, water freezes into ice and snow so none comes up through the roots. The water inside the soft leaves of broadleaf trees freezes too, and kills the leaves. So the trees sort of plan ahead by going dormant (kind of like taking a long nap) before winter, but first they get rid of their leaves and stop making food. As the leaves die, this process creates a beautiful show of color, especially where different tree species grow together, such as in the eastern forests of North America. You'll learn more about this process in the Eastern Forests section on page 11.

Many different types of forests can be found all over the world. What you see in them will depend on where you are and when you visit. Use this book to learn about many of the plants and animals that make the forest their home.

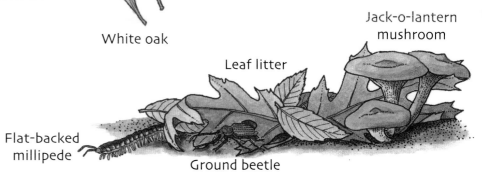

Jack-o-lantern mushroom

Leaf litter

Flat-backed millipede

Ground beetle

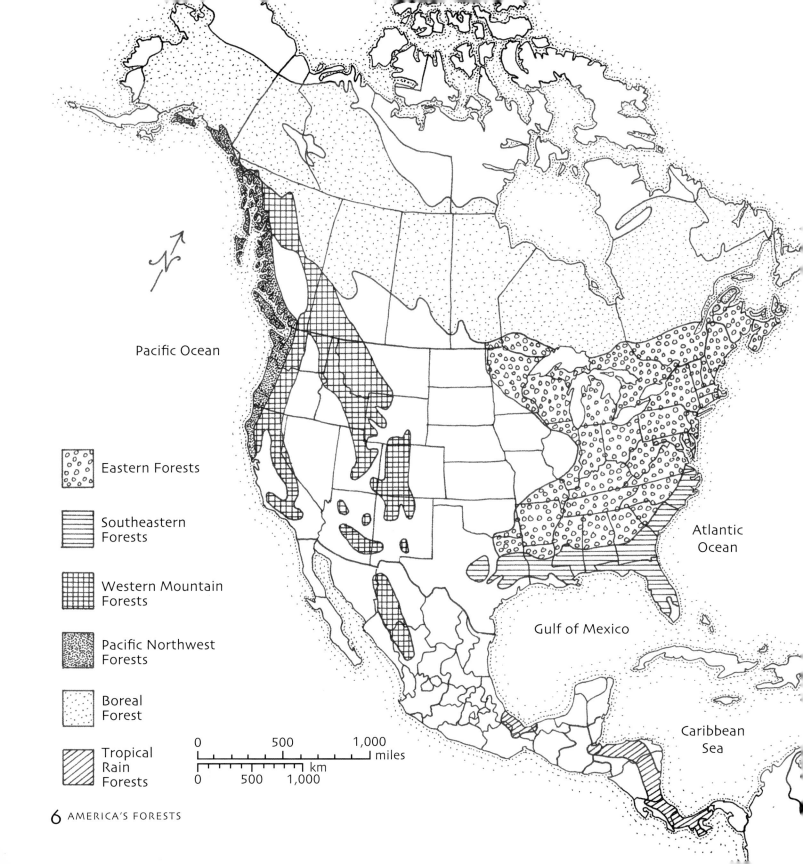

Pacific Ocean

Atlantic Ocean

Gulf of Mexico

Caribbean Sea

Eastern Forests

Southeastern Forests

Western Mountain Forests

Pacific Northwest Forests

Boreal Forest

Tropical Rain Forests

0　　　500　　　1,000
miles
0　　500　　1,000
km

North American Forests

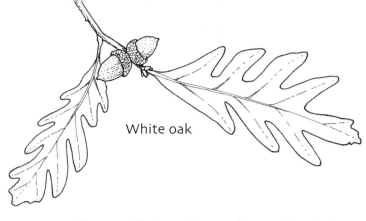

White oak

Forests are found in most of North America. This book will introduce you to some of the common plants and animals in six forest regions: Eastern Forests, Southeastern Forests, Western Mountain Forests, Pacific Northwest Forests, Boreal Forest, and Tropical Rain Forests.

These forests are not all the same. The boreal forest is made up of mostly spruce trees and other conifers that survive the bitter cold and snow of very long winters. In the cool rain and fog of the Pacific Northwest, huge **western hemlocks** and **redwoods** grow from a shady fern- and moss-covered forest floor. And in the forests of the East, there are more types, or species, of deciduous hardwoods, such as maples and oaks, than anywhere else in North America.

Why do different trees grow in different areas? Some reasons are the differences in high and low temperatures, the available water, and the type of soil. Another reason is fire. Certain trees can survive a forest fire better or grow back more quickly than others. There are even some pine trees whose cones won't open and release seeds unless they've been heated by fire.

All forests grow, or develop, over a long period of time. A large fire, a strong storm, or people cutting down trees can all leave open ground where a forest once stood. The first plants to return to this open area are sun-loving plants like grasses and flowers. Their seeds may float on the wind or come out of the poop of local seed-eating animals. Shrubs, young trees, and other low plants also take advantage of the sunshine. If the weather is warm and there is lots of water, plants will grow over the area quickly. If it is cold or dry, it will take longer for the plants to grow. During this change, called **succession**, the large, taller trees become established once more and the area becomes a **climax forest**. Some forests have never burned or been cut down. These **virgin forests**, often found in national parks and other protected areas, are full of trees that are many hundreds of years old.

Forests are not made up of just trees and plants, of course. Animals live there too. Birds build nests on tree branches or in tree trunks. Bears eat forest plants and sleep in hollow logs. And squirrels, mice, raccoons, and deer are some of the animals that eat the **mast**, or seeds and acorns that grow on trees and fall to the ground.

Deer mouse and acorns

In many places of North America, a forest is nearby. Explore and learn what makes your forest area special.

North American Forests

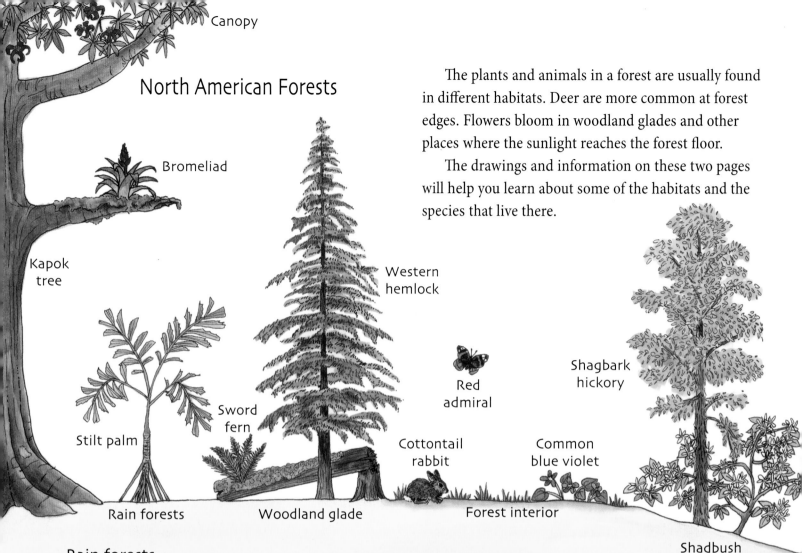

Canopy

Bromeliad

Kapok tree

Western hemlock

Shagbark hickory

Stilt palm

Sword fern

Red admiral

Cottontail rabbit

Common blue violet

Rain forests

Woodland glade

Forest interior

Shadbush

The plants and animals in a forest are usually found in different habitats. Deer are more common at forest edges. Flowers bloom in woodland glades and other places where the sunlight reaches the forest floor.

The drawings and information on these two pages will help you learn about some of the habitats and the species that live there.

Rain forests—

These are very wet forests where rain is common. Ferns and mosses may cover the forest floor, while bromeliads and other **epiphytes**, or air plants, can be found growing on the branches of trees. Tree leaves, vines, and other plants are often so thick that the forest floor is dark with shade.

Woodland glade—

These openings in the forest are often caused by trees that have fallen down. Once sunshine reaches the ground, grasses, flowers, and other sun-loving species begin to grow. Cottontail rabbits eat the soft, green plants found here, and butterflies visit the flowers.

Forest interior—

This is where trees grow closest together. Shrubs that can grow in shade, such as shadbush, are found beneath the trees in the shrub layer. Fallen branches and leaves create places for deer mice, snakes, beetles, and other animals to hide or search for food.

Canopy—

The canopy of tropical rain forest trees is home to animals such as howler and spider monkeys. Farther north, Clark's nutcrackers and the northern hawk owl are birds that sit high in the canopy of conifers in the United States and Canada. Since the forest canopy can be hard to see through all the leaves and branches, you may only hear the animals that spend time there.

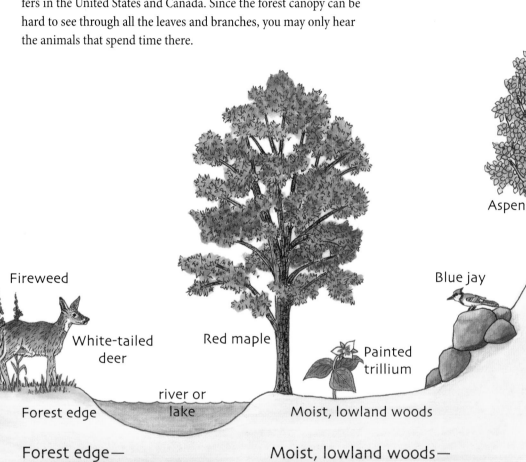

Clark's nutcracker

Ponderosa pine

Black bear

Mountains

Aspen

Blue jay

Fireweed

White-tailed deer

Red maple

Painted trillium

river or lake

Forest edge

Moist, lowland woods

Mountains—

Mountain forests can be cold places, especially in winter. And they are often drier than nearby valleys and lowlands. The low temperatures and lack of water create a more open forest habitat with trees that grow farther apart and with fewer shrubs. This makes it easier to spot the black bears that are common residents among the pines, firs, and other conifers.

Forest edge—

Fireweed and other sun-loving flowers, shrubs, and trees grow along the forest's edge. Unlike a woodland glade, which will eventually fill in with new trees, the edge of the forest is always open to sunlight. Look for deer eating the many leaves and small plants that are found here.

Moist, lowland woods—

The damp, rich soil near rivers and lakes is the best place to look for moisture-loving trees like hemlock and sweetgum and for elderberry shrubs. Skunk cabbage and corn-lily are also common here. And since blue jays and other birds eat elderberries, look for birds here too.

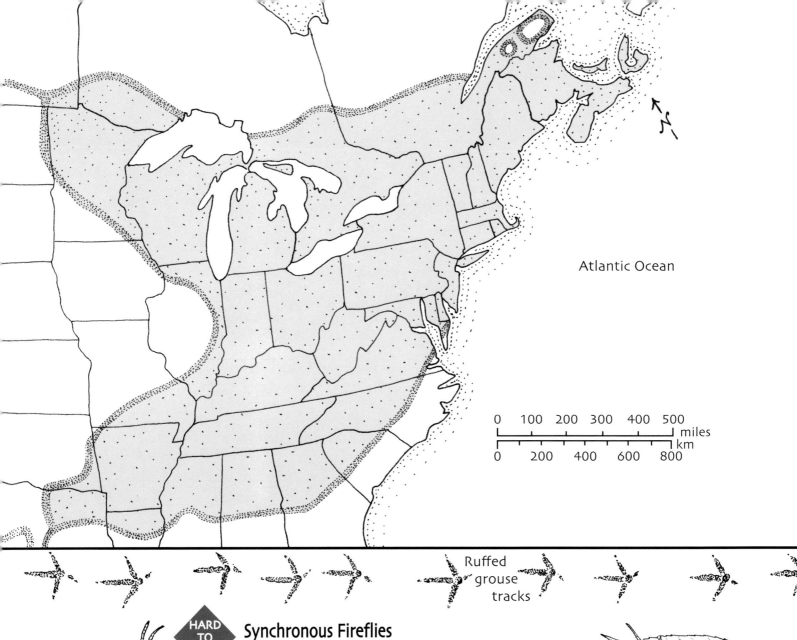

Atlantic Ocean

0 100 200 300 400 500
miles
km
0 200 400 600 800

Ruffed grouse tracks

Synchronous Fireflies

HARD TO FIND

Have you seen fireflies? Even if you don't live where fireflies, or lightning bugs, are found, you probably know about them. They are a type of beetle whose abdomen can light up, usually flashing on and off at night, mostly during the warmer weather of the year.

Now imagine hundreds of fireflies on a forest hillside or in a clearing all flashing on and off *at the same time*, or synchronously. During just two to three weeks in June, you can see this light show in some woodland areas of the southern Appalachian Mountains. It begins after dark and lasts for a couple hours.

Eastern Forests

Eastern forests are forests of changing seasons. In no other North American region are winter, spring, summer, and autumn so obvious.

Winter here is still, almost like the forest is sleeping. Since most of the trees and shrubs are deciduous and lose their leaves in the fall, winter is a good time to look for old squirrel nests (a ball of dead leaves), nest holes in tree trunks (used by different animals including squirrels and birds), or bird nests on branches. Make a note where you see these things. In spring, when baby birds and other animals may be using the nests, newly grown leaves make them hard to find again.

Spring begins quietly. You have to pay attention to notice some of the tiny buds of new leaves and flowers on the bare brown and gray branches of trees and shrubs. Check the ground for **trilliums**, **blue phlox**, and other wildflowers as they push up through the leaf litter and bloom in the warming sunlight.

By the end of spring, there is green everywhere. The leaves of **maple**, **hickory**, and other broad-leafed trees grow and open, shading the forest floor. **White-tailed deer** (also called whitetail deer) and **cottontail rabbits** move to forest edges or glades to find and eat the grasses and other fresh green leaves that grow where the sunlight still reaches the ground.

Summer is often hot and humid. Listen for the loud daytime buzzing sounds of **cicadas** and the evening chirping, clicking sounds of **katydids.** You may also hear the drumming of **woodpeckers** as they use their sharp bills to cut holes in tree bark to eat the beetles and other insects they find there.

When summer ends and the days become shorter and cooler, the forest prepares for its most amazing change. Deciduous trees and shrubs begin to shut down for the winter and the green color of chlorophyll, a chemical that helps make food for the tree, fades away. After the green is gone, the leaf's other colors—yellow, red, orange, purple, and so on, depending upon the type of tree—can be seen. Look for the bright yellow of **yellow-poplar**, the deep orange of **sugar maples** (whose sap is made into maple syrup), the reddish purple of **sweetgum**, and the red of **red maples**.

As you look at the illustrations on the next two pages, you'll see the three busiest forest seasons: spring on the left, summer in the middle, and autumn on the right. There is so much to see whenever you visit.

Tree squirrel nest

Cicada

Katydid

EASTERN FORESTS

Spring

Eastern hemlock

Bitternut hickory

Basswood

Cardinal

Yellow-poplar

White-tailed deer

Shagbark hickory

Rhododendron

Beech

Lady's slipper orchid

Blue jay

Dogwood

Wild turkey

Mayapple

Ruffed grouse

Redbud

Gray fox

Painted trillium

Virginia bluebells

Sweet joe-pye weed

Columbine

Jack-in-the-pulpit

Spotted salamander

Chipmunk

Blue phlox

Fall

Red admiral

Eastern white pine

Sugar maple

Red maple

Falcate orangetip

Fox squirrel

Red oak

Yellow birch

Witch-hazel

Red fox

Cinnamon fern

Raccoon

White-breasted nuthatch

Shadbush

Gray Squirrel

Box turtle

Bobcat

Cottontail rabbit

Woodland sunflower

Polypody fern

Copperhead

Cardinal flower

Five-lined skink

Eyed click beetle

Spring peeper

Beaver

Wood frog

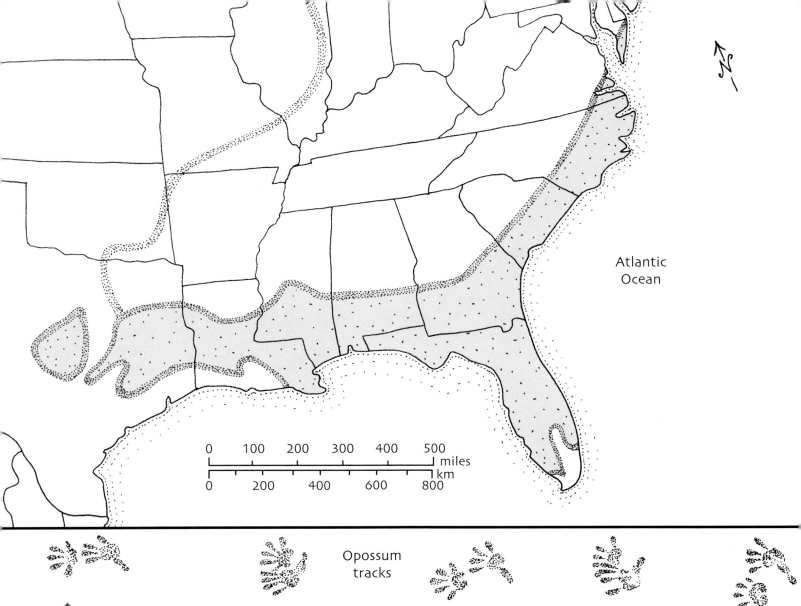

Atlantic
Ocean

| 0 | 100 | 200 | 300 | 400 | 500 |
miles
km
| 0 | 200 | 400 | 600 | 800 |

Opossum
tracks

HARD TO FIND ▶ Oak Toads

Listen for the peeping sound of baby birds or chicks at night. That may actually be the sound of oak toads, the smallest toads in North America. Their peeping is really loud when you are near them, but watch where you walk so you don't step on these tiny toads.

Look for oak toads during the day when they hunt insects and spiders on the sandy soil beneath pine and oak trees. Their grayish bodies blend in with the sand, so they are easier to see when they are moving. Oak toads also have a light stripe down their back and red or orange warts.

Actual size

Southeastern Forests

These are the forests of the coastal plain, land that gently slopes down toward the Atlantic Ocean and the Gulf of Mexico.

Pines are one of the most common types of tree here. They grow on dry, sandy hills and low, flat, sandy soil. **Longleaf pine** is one of the easiest to identify. It has a tall, straight trunk and gets its name from its really long needles (the leaves of pine trees), which grow up to 18 inches (45.7 cm) long.

Fire is an important part of the pine forests. Many fires begin from lightning strikes. Lightning hits these forests more than any other region in North America. Fires may kill the small shrubs and trees, but the larger pines usually survive. This maintains a type of savannah, an open woodland that's a perfect place for newly fallen pine seeds to sprout into young trees.

Live oak and **magnolia** trees are also common in these forests, especially in the warmer southern part of the region. Live oaks are hard to miss. Their huge branches often begin low to the ground and grow out 50 feet (15.3 m) or more from the center of the tree. Look near the edges of ponds and swamps for magnolias. They have very large fragrant white flowers and shiny, dark green leaves.

Golden silk orb weaver

Actual size

Draped over the branches of many of these trees is a gray-green plant called **Spanish moss**. This is not really a moss but an epiphyte that gets all its water and food from rain and whatever is in the air.

In some areas, especially near plants such as longleaf pine, **turkey oak,** and **saw palmetto**, you may see a large hole in the sandy ground. That could be a **gopher tortoise** burrow. The burrow tunnel is usually 20 to 30 feet (6.1 to 9.2 m) long and provides a home for other animals as well, such as mice, rabbits, foxes, opossums, lizards, toads, frogs, insects, and snakes, both when the tortoise is still there and after the tortoise has abandoned it.

Do you like walking through spiderwebs? If not, then watch out for the large yellowish webs of the **golden silk orb weaver** in midsummer to early fall. This big brown and yellowish orange spider of open woodlands weaves an orb web that may be more than 3 feet (0.9 m) across!

Whether you walk among the pine trees or duck under swaying Spanish moss, you'll see a lot that's interesting and new here along the coastal plain.

Gopher tortoise

SOUTHEASTERN FORESTS

Opossum

Yellow-poplar

Sassafras

Red maple

Southern magnolia

Slash pine

Robin

White-tailed deer

Polypody fern

Poison ivy

Mayapple

Turkey beard

Pepperbush

Striped skunk

Armadillo

Wood duck

Trumpet creeper

Hummingbird

Fire pink

Green treefrog

Corn snake

Bird-foot violet

Live oak

Summer tanager

White oak

Longleaf pine

Gray squirrel

Spanish moss

Gray fox

Sweetgum

Persimmon

Pileated woodpecker

Turkey oak

Golden silk orb weaver

Saw palmetto

Raccoon

Wild turkey

Wiregrass

Cabbage palmetto

Cottontail rabbit

Huckleberry

Fox squirrel

Broadhead skink

Horned devil

Northern bobwhite

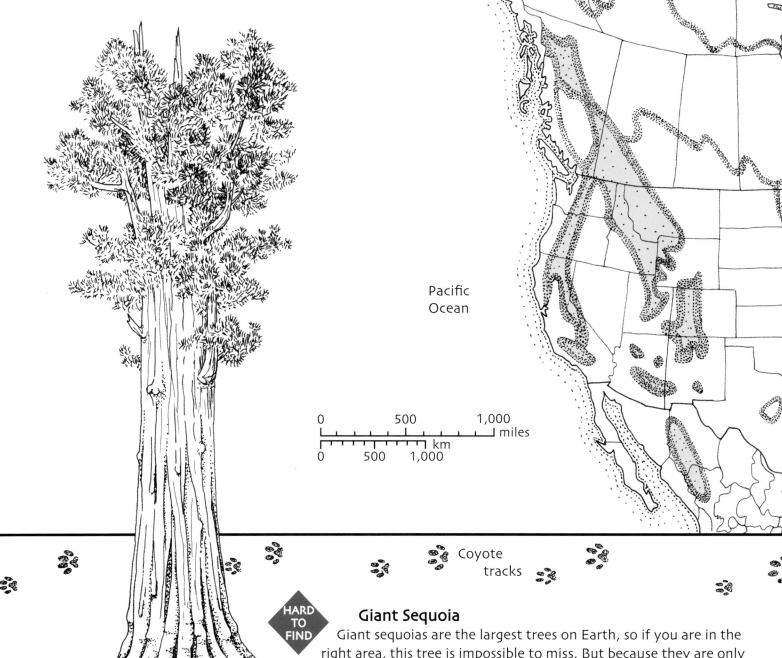

Pacific
Ocean

0	500	1,000

miles

km

| 0 | 500 | 1,000 |

Coyote
tracks

◆ **HARD TO FIND**

Giant Sequoia

Giant sequoias are the largest trees on Earth, so if you are in the right area, this tree is impossible to miss. But because they are only found in a few protected places, you have to make a special journey to see them. Most are found in Sequoia and Kings Canyon national parks in California. And since many giant sequoias are 2,000 to 3,000 years old, they are some of the oldest trees on Earth as well.

The biggest of these already huge trees is called General Sherman. It is 275 feet (83.8 m) tall with a circumference (the distance around the trunk) of 102$\frac{1}{2}$ feet (31.2 m)!

Western Mountain Forests

These forests are found on the slopes of the Rocky Mountains, the Cascades, and the Sierra Nevada. They are open forests that are shaped by dry weather and fire where conifers are common. Dead pine needles may litter the forest floor. Walking on them can be slippery, so be careful.

In the spring, water that was frozen as snow or ice melts and flows into creeks and meadows. **Iris** and **shooting stars** flower in moist, sunny glades. In early summer, bright pink **fireweed** grows along roadsides and other open spaces. Meadows and the margins of streams often stay moist throughout the summer. Look there for red **Indian paintbrush** and purple or blue **lupines**.

If you're in a forest with **ponderosa pines**, check the base of the trees for pinkish, sticky, fuzzy-looking flower stalks sticking straight up and out of the pine needles. Those are **pinedrops**. They have no green chlorophyll, so the plant can't make its own food. Instead, the roots of pinedrops get nutrients through the soil from the roots of the nearby pine trees.

Near ponderosa pines but a bit higher up the mountain is the similar-looking Jeffrey pine. Walk up to one of these trees and put your nose into a crack on the scaly, reddish brown bark. You'll probably smell vanilla (although some people say it is more like pineapple).

But wait! Don't leave these pine forests yet. Look around on the ground. Do you see scattered pieces of pine cones? This is the work of **tassel-eared squirrels** or other tree squirrels. They pull off the cone scales to eat the seeds and soft food inside.

The blue **Steller's jay** is a common, loud bird that's hard to miss here. It is bold and will often steal food from campsites and picnic tables. Another loud, bold jay that also steals food is the **Clark's nutcracker**, although this gray and black bird is more commonly seen high in the mountains, calling and flying from treetop to treetop.

As the summer fades and fall arrives, the leaves of **aspen** trees turn golden yellow. Fall is also the time when male **elk**, also called wapiti, challenge each other with a loud call. This bugle can be heard for great distances in forests like those at Yellowstone National Park.

So do you like open forests and pine trees and views of wildlife, moist meadows, and mountain wildflowers? If you do, then grab a hiking stick, put on your boots, and enjoy your time exploring these great mountain forests.

Tassel-eared squirrel

Ponderosa pine

Pinedrops

WESTERN MOUNTAIN FORESTS

Gray jay

Douglas-fir

Black bear

White fur

Engelmann spruce

Elk

Fireweed

Corn-lily

Cow parsnip

Willow

White-tailed deer

Raccoon

Mountain-ash

Shooting star

Columbine

Bobcat

Indian paintbrush

Iris

Garter snake

Ten-lined June beetle

Wild strawberry

Carpenter ant

Cottontail rabbit

Clark's nutcracker

Steller's jay

Lodgepole pine

Western gray squirrel

Tiger swallowtail

Sugar pine

Ponderosa pine

Coyote

Aspen

White-breasted nuthatch

Mule deer

Chickadee

Heartleaf arnica

Wild rose

Red squirrel

Lupine

Chipmunk

Golden-mantled ground squirrel

Blue grouse

Dark-eyed junco

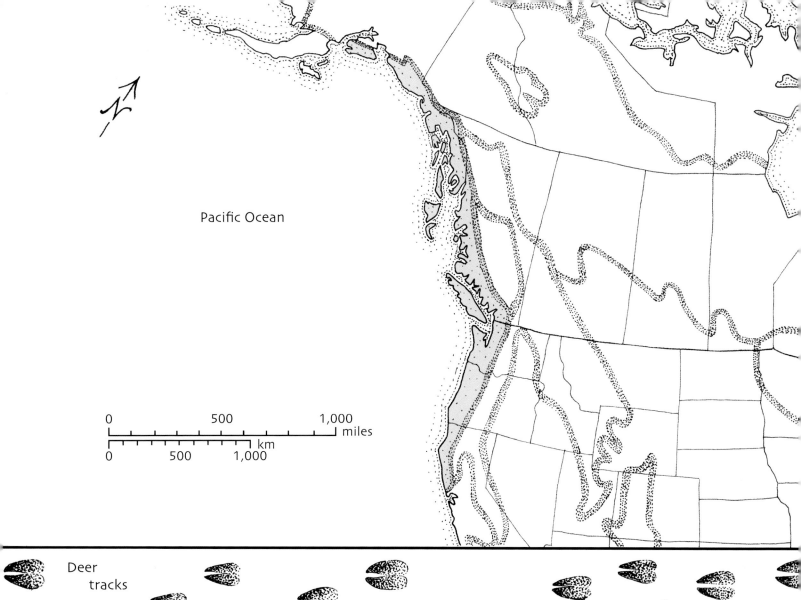

Pacific Ocean

0	500	1,000
miles

km

| 0 | 500 | 1,000 |

Deer tracks

HARD TO FIND

Red Tree Voles

These little reddish mice- or ratlike animals live most of their lives in trees, usually Douglas-fir. They use pee and dried poop in their nests to hold together lichen, small branches, and other plant material. The voles eat the needles, or leaves, of the Douglas-fir and other conifers and drink the water they lick off the leaves. Since they are nocturnal, or active at night, and live above the ground, you'll probably have better luck finding their nests rather than the voles themselves.

Pacific Northwest Forests

Damp, dark, quiet forests are what you'll find here. The ground is cushiony from fallen leaves, mosses, and lichens. Cool mist and fog blow in from the Pacific Ocean, and rain is common.

It is here in the Pacific Northwest, in Washington's Olympic National Park, that you will find the Hoh Rain Forest. Unlike the hot tropical rain forests, the Hoh is a northern **temperate** rain forest and has much cooler temperatures. Even in summer, it is usually below 80°F (26.4°C). And it gets lots and lots of rain—from 140 to 167 inches (355.6 to 424.2 cm) each year.

Deep in some of the forests of this region are lichens that drape from the branches of trees and shrubs. They look a bit like strands of grayish hair, which might be why they are called **old man's beard** or **witch's hair**.

Do you see any trees growing in a straight line? They probably began life on a **nurse log**, a fallen tree whose moss-covered rotting wood provided the perfect place for the tree seeds to grow. Eventually the fallen log will rot away, leaving just the row of new trees.

Douglas-fir, **Sitka spruce**, and **western red cedar** are among the trees that grow to great size and age in these forests. Many are over 200 feet (61.0 m) tall

Old man's beard

and hundreds of years old, especially in places protected from storms and from people cutting them down for wood.

The record holder for the tallest tree in the world is also here in the Pacific Northwest: a 370-foot (112.8-m) **redwood**. Most redwoods grow in the southern part of the forests along the California coast and can be more than 2,000 years old.

Their huge reddish brown trunks often rise up from a fern-covered forest floor. You have to lean your head way back just to see the lowest branches. Try to visit the redwoods in the spring when the **rhododendrons** are in bloom. These bushes of pink flowers add nice color to the shady green and brown forest.

Look for slimy **banana slugs** along the trails. They are usually pale to bright yellow, like a banana. They grow to about 10 inches (25.4 cm) long and are the second largest slug in the world. (A slug from Europe is a little bit larger.)

The dense green forests and giant old trees of this coastal region are hard to describe in words. They seem almost prehistoric. You'll have to visit and experience them for yourself.

Redwood

PACIFIC NORTHWEST FORESTS

Douglas-fir

Rhododendron

Redwood

Douglas' squirrel

Elk

Lady fern

Red elderberry

Ocean spray

Bigleaf maple

Devil's club

Club moss

Tiger swallowtail

Western trillium

Calypso orchid

Chipmunk

Red huckleberry

Bunchberry

Redwood sorrel

Dark-eyed junco

Skunk cabbage

Steller's jay

Silver fir

Black bear

Western red cedar

Varied thrush

Red alder

Western hemlock and seedling

Sitka spruce

Vine maple

Black-tailed deer

Sword fern

Amanita mushroom

Salmonberry

Salal

Banana slug

Sooty grouse

Stair-step moss

Yellow-spotted millipede

Rough-skinned newt

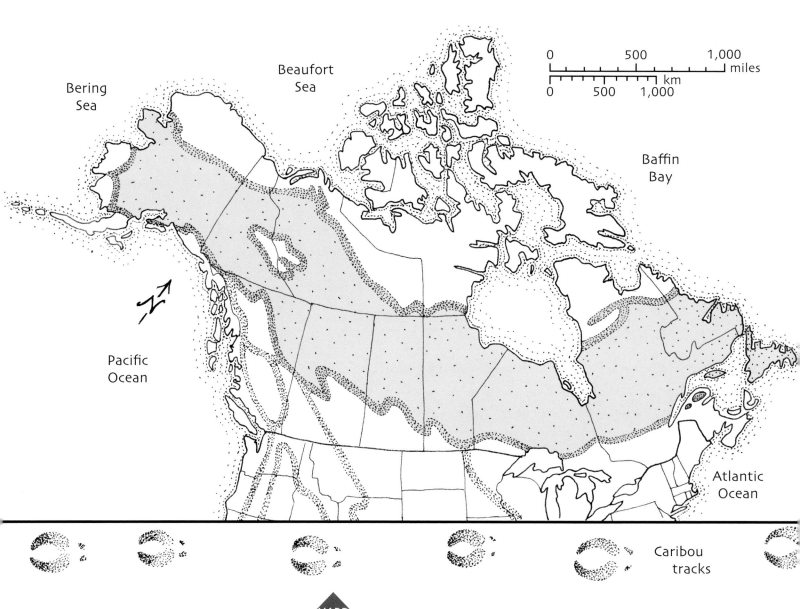

Bering
Sea

Beaufort
Sea

Baffin
Bay

Pacific
Ocean

Atlantic
Ocean

0	500	1,000

miles

0	500	1,000

km

Caribou
tracks

HARD TO FIND

Wolverine

You may not want to find this shy animal. The wolverine is very strong and can be fierce—it can even scare bears away from animals the bears have killed. Wolverines eat almost anything, dead or alive. That's probably why some people call them glutton, which means someone who eats too much. Another name for them is skunk bear because they look like a mix of a small bear and a skunk and can leave a strong smell.

Wolverines are 3 to 4 feet (0.9 to 1.2 m) long and the second largest member of the weasel family. (Sea otters are the largest.)

Boreal Forest

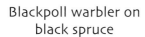

Blackpoll warbler on black spruce

Imagine a forest so large that you can walk for hundreds of miles in any direction and still be in the same forest. That is the boreal forest, or taiga, of North America, the largest continuous forest in the world.

This is one of the coldest places on Earth. Winter can last for more than six months with temperatures below -50°F (-46°C). Even in summer, it rarely gets above 70°F (21°C).

In many areas, the ground stays frozen within a few feet of the surface all year long. This permafrost prevents tree roots from growing deep into the ground. As the surface thaws in warm weather and freezes in cold weather, small hills and low spots form. This sometimes causes the shallow-rooted trees that grow here to tilt into what is called a drunken forest.

The most common trees in the boreal forest are **spruce**, **fir**, and other conifers. Many of these have a pointed-cone shape that keeps snow from building up on the trees in winter and breaking the branches.

Mosquito

When warm weather arrives and much of the snow and ice melt, low shrubs such as **squashberry** and **twinflower** grow quickly on the forest floor. Small groups of **woodland caribou** move through the forest eating **caribou moss**, a type of lichen. And you may see **moose**, the largest member of the deer family, standing in shallow ponds and lakes eating the water plants that grow there.

Mosses are common and cover layers of dead twigs and conifer needles on the forest floor, making the ground feel soft and spongy. Throughout the forest, you will find old ponds and lakes called bogs. **Sphagnum moss** often covers the bog, and **tamarack** trees grow along the edge.

Sparrows, **warblers**, and other birds take advantage of the warmer weather too. They migrate here in late spring to lay eggs, raise their young, and feast on the growing plants and insects, such as **mosquitoes**. More than one and a half billion birds breed in the boreal forest (yes, that's *billion*). And if you include shorebirds, ducks, and other birds that use the ponds and lakes within the forest, the number is even higher. To write it another way, about one-third of all birds in North America have their babies in this forest.

Although many plant and animal species are the same throughout the boreal forest, some are more common in the western or eastern regions. So in the scene on the next two pages, the more western plants and animals are on the left and the more eastern species are on the right.

Enjoy exploring the boreal forest.

BOREAL FOREST

Balsam fir

White spruce

Bald eagle

Black bear

Paper birch

Porcupine

Boreal owl

Moose

Aspen

Chickadee

Balsam poplar

Lynx

River otter

Labrador tea

Snowshoe hare

Beaver lodge

Spruce grouse

Bunchberry

Wood frog

Squashberry

Canada violet

White-throated sparrow

Fireweed

Northern hawk owl

Pine grosbeak

Great gray owl

Northern goshawk

Jack pine

Pink-edged sulphur

Black spruce

Crossbill

Gray wolf

Gray jay

Red squirrel

Tamarack

Black-backed woodpecker

Red fox

Reindeer moss

Caribou

Red-breasted nuthatch

Lady fern

Gooseberry

Bead lily

Marten

Red-backed vole

Twinflower

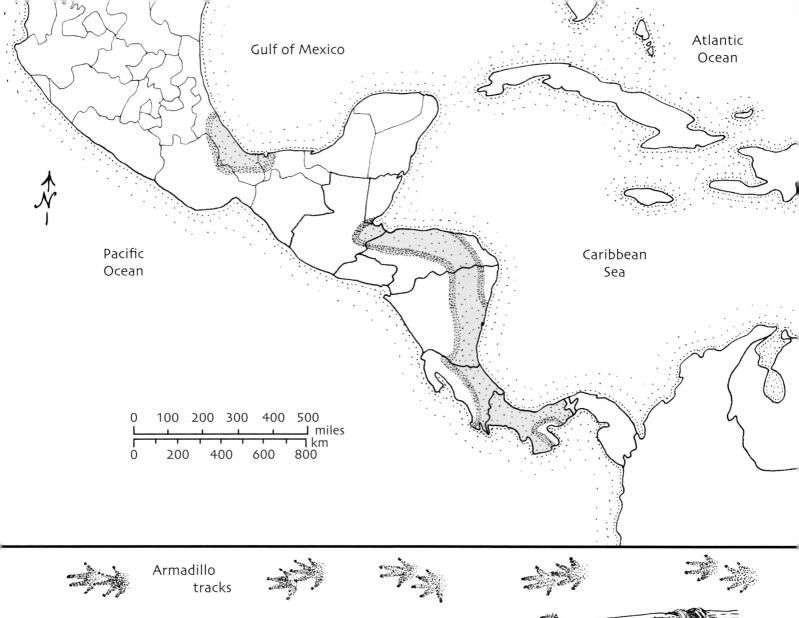

Gulf of Mexico

Atlantic Ocean

Pacific Ocean

Caribbean Sea

| 0 | 100 | 200 | 300 | 400 | 500 |
miles
km
| 0 | 200 | 400 | 600 | 800 |

Armadillo tracks

HARD TO FIND

Sloths

Sloths are very slow-moving animals. They spend almost all their time hanging upside down, gripping a tree trunk or branch with their long, curved claws and eating mostly leaves. Even though they can get pretty big, up to 2½ feet (0.8 m) long, their grayish or brown fur blends in with the shadows of the rain forest. Sloths only come down onto the forest floor about once a week—to poop.

Tropical Rain Forests

Green iguana on liana

Hot and wet. That is how many describe these lowland tropical rain forests. And with good reason: the average temperature is 86˚F (30˚C) and it receives 156 to 312 inches (396.2 to 792.5 cm) of rainfall each year.

The canopy of this forest is so dense that from the air it looks like a solid layer of green trees. In some areas, only 1 percent of the sunlight gets through to the ground. Yet many plants and animals thrive in the 200 feet (61.0 m) of jungle from the canopy to the shady forest floor. As a matter of fact, the lowland tropical rain forests of the world have more plant and animal species than any other habitat on Earth.

A large lizard called the **green iguana** spends most of its time in the forest canopy. **Howler monkeys** are also found in the canopy. Listen for this monkey's loud call. It can be heard in the morning and just before dark at a distance of up to 2 or 3 miles (3 to 5 km) away.

Colorful **bromeliads** grow on branches above the forest floor, getting water and food from rain and the air around them. These epiphytes, or "air plants," are home to many small rain forest animals. **Tarantulas** live on bromeliads, and **dink frogs**, which have a bell-like call, live in the water held by the center leaves.

In the shady darkness of the forest floor, trails of **leafcutter ants** carry bits of leaves back to their nest. A fungus will grow on the leaves and become food for the ant colony.

And huge numbers of **army ants**, in groups of 30,000 to 1,000,000, spread forward in columns, catching and killing all insects and other small animals in their path.

Be careful where you step in this forest. The **terciopelo**, or **fer-de-lance**, a poisonous snake colored like dead brown leaves, is often seen along trails. But if you're lucky, you may spot another brownish animal in the deep shade of the forest, one of the largest butterflies in the world, the **owl butterfly**, with a wingspan of 5 inches (12.7 cm).

Stop along a trail and look up. Do you see what looks like thick ropes growing up tree trunks and across branches from tree to tree? Those are woody vines called **lianas**.

Lots of birds live in the tropical rain forest. Some of the largest and most colorful are **scarlet macaws** and **toucans**. One type of toucan is black with a yellow bill and is sometimes called a flying banana. When you visit this amazing place, wear rubber boots to walk through the mud and protect your feet from biting insects. And expect to get wet, because, after all, this is a *rain* forest.

Leafcutter ant

TROPICAL RAIN FORESTS

Spider monkey

Scarlet macaws

Monkey ladder

Rubber tree

Blue morpho butterfly

Toucan

Monstera

Cebus monkey

Strangler fig

Orange-chinned parakeet

Dink frog

Acacia

Bromeliad

Whiptail lizard

Tarantula

Heliconia

Agouti

Blue jeans dart frog

Hummingbird

Kapok tree

Bat

Cecropia tree

Elephant ear philodendron

Howler monkey

Lianas

Stilt palm

Owl butterflies

Pale-billed woodpecker

Fishtail palm

Anteater

Coati

Peanut-head bug

Passionflower

Terciopelo

Monkey pot tree seed pod

Armadillo

Spanish flag orchid

Leaf-mimic katydid

Hercules beetle

Common Plants and Animals

Although there are many differences among North American forests, the forests share many of the same types of plants and animals. On the following pages, you will see drawings and information about many of these common species.

To have the best luck finding forest plants and animals, learn *when* to look as well as *where* to look. For example, forest flowers are most common during the spring in places where sunlight reaches the forest floor. And animals such as turkeys, squirrels, and white-tailed deer all eat the acorns from oak trees, so you may see these animals near oaks when the acorns ripen in the fall.

You also need to listen in a forest. Many of the birds, insects, and other forest animals are hidden among the leaves and branches of trees and shrubs, making them hard to see. Others, like frogs, hide during the day but begin calling after sunset, so you may find these animals by first hearing their calls or the other sounds they make.

The more you look around you, the more you'll discover.

MICE

Color: Most are rusty brown to grayish on top and white underneath.
Size: Usually 5–8 inches (12.7–20.3 cm) long. (That includes the tail.)
Food: Seeds, fruit, and insects.
Notes: Mice are probably the most common forest mammals, but since they're nocturnal, you'd have to be out at night—and be quiet and very still—to see them running around. Mice are food for owls, foxes, bobcats, and snakes.

ROBIN

Color: Brown on back with black head and reddish breast.
Size: 10 inches (25.4 cm) long.
Food: Worms, insects, berries, and other small fruit.
Notes: Robins are found almost everywhere in North America where there are trees, grass, or meadows. Look for them near open areas, often on the ground hunting for worms. It is the state bird of Connecticut, Michigan, and Wisconsin.

TREE SQUIRRELS

Color: Red and Douglas' squirrels are reddish. Gray and fox squirrels are gray to reddish brown or reddish gray. Black-colored gray or fox squirrels may also be seen. All have lighter colors underneath.
Size: Body length ranges from about 10½–15 inches (26.7–38.1 cm) for the small red and Douglas' squirrels and up to 23 inches (58.4 cm) for the gray squirrel. The fox squirrel is the largest tree squirrel and can have a body length of 28 inches (71.1 cm).
Food: Nuts, pine cones, bark, flowers, fruit, fungi such as mushrooms, and sometimes insects.
Notes: Tree squirrels often store nuts by burying them in the ground. Some nuts are never eaten and may grow into trees. Tree squirrels use their bushy tails for balance, shade, and a blanket when it is cold. To find squirrels, listen for the barking or chattering noises they make, or watch for them running on the forest floor and up and down tree trunks. The gray squirrel is the state mammal of North Carolina, and the state wild game animal of Kentucky.

ASPEN

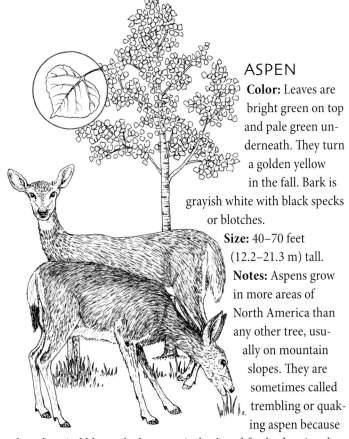

Color: Leaves are bright green on top and pale green underneath. They turn a golden yellow in the fall. Bark is grayish white with black specks or blotches.

Size: 40–70 feet (12.2–21.3 m) tall.

Notes: Aspens grow in more areas of North America than any other tree, usually on mountain slopes. They are sometimes called trembling or quaking aspen because when the wind blows, the leaves twist back and forth, showing the bright and pale green colors. This makes it look like the whole tree is shaking.

MULE DEER AND WHITE-TAILED DEER

Color: Both types of deer are mostly grayish brown with white on their undersides.

Size: $4^1/_2$–$5^1/_2$ feet (1.4–1.7 m) high.

Food: Grasses and leaves of bushes and trees.

Notes: Look for deer near the edges of forests in the early morning or late afternoon. You might even see them along roads at night, visible from the car's headlights. The white-tailed deer is named for the white underside of its tail that shows when the deer runs away from danger. It is the state mammal of Arkansas, Illinois, Michigan, Nebraska, New Hampshire, Ohio, Pennsylvania, and South Carolina, and the state game animal of Oklahoma.

CARPENTER ANTS

Color: Most are black, brown, or reddish.

Size: $^1/_8$–$^1/_2$ inch (0.3–1.3 cm) long, depending on the species.

Food: Insects and plant juices.

Notes: Carpenter ants nest in tunnels they dig out of trees that have fallen or been cut down. Since they look for food at night, that's when you will probably see them walking around. The giant carpenter ant is the biggest ant in North America.

CHICKADEE

Color: Light gray or brownish and white. Black on top of head and on throat. White cheeks.

Size: 4–5 inches (10.2–12.7 cm) long.

Food: Insects, spiders, seeds, and berries.

Notes: This common little bird is often seen on trees near picnic areas and campgrounds. It is the state bird of Maine and Massachusetts, and the provincial bird of New Brunswick.

DARK-EYED JUNCO

Color: Usually grayish brown with a black head. Some have gray heads.

Size: 6 inches (15.2 cm) from beak to tail.

Food: Seeds and insects.

Notes: These little birds hop about on the ground looking for food. They are commonly seen in campgrounds and picnic areas.

Birds

JAYS

Color: Blue jays are blue with black and white on their faces and gray breasts. Steller's jays are blue and black. And gray jays are…gray!

Size: About 11 inches (27.9 cm) long.

Food: Jays will eat almost anything; however, seeds, nuts, and insects are their main foods.

Notes: Jays can be noisy birds; you may hear their calls before you see them. The Steller's jay is common at campsites and picnic areas in western forests. It is the provincial bird of British Columbia. The blue jay is the provincial bird of Prince Edward Island.

Steller's jay

Gray jay

Blue jay

BLUEBIRD

Color: Male is bright blue with reddish breast and white belly.

Size: 7 inches (17.8 cm) long.

Food: Insects and small fruits.

Notes: Look for bluebirds in forests and woodlands, usually next to open areas. They nest in tree holes. Bluebirds are found across most of North America. The bluebird is the state bird of Missouri and New York.

CARDINAL

Color: Red males. Tan and red females.

Size: Almost 9 inches (22.9 cm) long.

Food: Seeds, fruit, and insects.

Notes: Found in woodland edges, often near water. The red color makes this bird pretty easy to spot. The cardinal is the state bird of Illinois, Indiana, Kentucky, North Carolina, Ohio, Virginia, and West Virginia.

Northern flicker

Pileated woodpecker

Downy woodpecker

WOODPECKERS

Color: Usually black and white. Northern flickers are black and tan. Most males and some females have red on their heads. Look for yellow or pale orange underneath the flickers' wings as they fly.

Size: The large pileated woodpecker is about $16^1/_2$ inches (41.9 cm) long, the downy is 7 inches (17.8 cm) long, and the northern flicker is about $12^1/_2$ inches (31.8 cm) long.

Food: Mostly insects dug out of tree bark. Pileated woodpeckers eat carpenter ants from dead trees. Flickers eat insects they find on the ground.

Notes: Listen for the sound of hammering as woodpeckers chip holes in trees. Small holes are used to hunt for food. Large holes are used to live in.

WILD TURKEY

Color: Dark brown. Males have red on their heads.

Size: The males are 46 inches (1.2 m) long. The females are about 37 inches (0.9 m) long.

Food: Seeds, nuts, fruit, leaves, and roots. When turkeys are very young, they eat insects.

Notes: Look for turkeys in forest glades or openings. They are also seen along the forest's edge. In springtime, the male's gobble can be heard up to a mile away. The wild turkey is the state game bird of Alabama, Massachusetts, Oklahoma, and South Carolina.

Arthropods (Insects and Their Relatives)

KATYDID

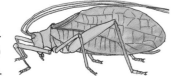

Color: Mostly green. Some species are brown, tan, or pink.
Size: Up to 2½ inches (6.4 cm) long, depending on the species.
Food: Leaves. Some species eat insects.
Notes: Katydids have color and wing patterns that blend in with forest leaves, so they may be hard to spot. Find them by listening for the buzzing, clicking, chirping, or "katy-DID" sounds they make.

CICADA

Color: Most are brown or blackish with green or orange. All have clear wings.
Size: Commonly 1–2 inches (2.5–5.1 cm) long.
Food: Tree sap and other plant juices, depending on the species. The young live underground and suck juices from plant roots.
Notes: You may not see cicadas, but you'll definitely hear them. Listen for loud (sometimes very loud!) buzzing sounds on hot afternoons in the summer.

WOLF SPIDER

Color: Brownish.
Size: Body is about ½ inch (1.3 cm) long; they are 1 inch (2.5 cm) long including the legs.
Food: Insects.
Notes: You'll find this spider among the fallen leaves on the forest floor. To find it at night, use a flashlight—the wolf spider's eyes will shine silver from the light.

BUTTERFLIES and MOTHS

Color: Many different colors. Moths are usually not as colorful as butterflies.
Size: The tiger swallowtail and polyphemus moth both have wingspans up to 5½ inches (14 cm). Most butterflies and moths are much smaller.
Food: Flower nectar.
Notes: Butterflies are diurnal, which means they're out during the day. Moths, however, are nocturnal, so look for them at night. A swallowtail is the state butterfly of Alabama, Arizona, Delaware, Georgia, Mississippi, Oklahoma, South Carolina, and Tennessee, and the state insect of Oregon and Virginia.

Tiger swallowtail

Polyphemus moth

DADDY LONGLEGS or HARVESTMAN

Color: Black or brownish.
Size: Body is ¼–³/₈ inch (0.6–1.0 cm) long. Legs are very long and skinny.
Food: Insects and plants.
Notes: Daddy longlegs are related to spiders. Look for them walking on tree trunks at night or among plants near the cool, damp forest floor during the day, especially during the summer and fall.

WOOD-BORING BEETLES and BARK BEETLES

Color: Often shiny black or brown, sometimes metallic green, blue, copper, or brown.
Size: Ranges from the 1-inch (2.5 cm) wood-boring beetles to the tiny ¼-inch (0.6 cm) bark beetles.
Food: Young beetles (larvae) will eat the wood of trees. Adults may eat wood or other plant material.
Notes: If you pull some bark off dead trees, you may notice trails or holes these beetles have made. You may even see the beetle or its wormlike larvae.

Mammals

BLACK BEAR

Color: Black or brown.

Size: 3–3½ feet (0.9–1.1 m) high when walking on all four feet.

Food: Berries, plants, honey, insects, fish, and other small animals.

Notes: Although black bears may be out any time of the day, you will probably spot them at night as they look for food. All types of bears are dangerous. Never walk toward or feed a bear, and always keep picnic and camping food packed away, out of sight in your car or in a bear-proof container. The black bear is the state animal of New Mexico.

RACCOON

Color: Brownish gray body. Tail has bands of tan and dark brown. Face has black mask surrounded by white.

Size: 2–3 feet (0.6–0.9 m) long.

Food: Almost anything, including seeds, fruit, insects, small mammals, and eggs.

Notes: Found in most North American forests. Raccoons are nocturnal, so you'll probably only see them at night. Watch for them near streams and along roads.

MOOSE

Color: Dark brown

Size: About 6½–7½ feet (2.0–2.3 m) tall.

Food: Usually shrubs and other plants found in or near water.

Notes: Moose are the largest of the hoofed animals and are in the deer family. Look for them walking through the forest near shallow lakes and ponds or standing in the water eating the plants growing there. Be careful: moose are unpredictable and may run at you if they get upset. The moose is the state land mammal of Alaska, and the state animal of Maine.

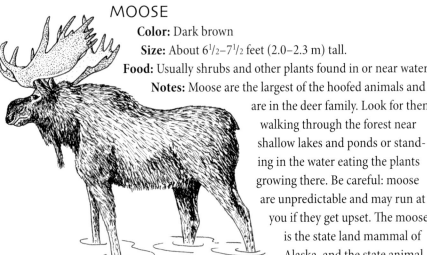

BOBCAT

Color: Yellowish brown with dark spots.

Size: Up to 15 inches (38.1 cm) high at the shoulder and 3½ feet (1.1 m) long.

Food: Rabbits, mice, squirrels, and other medium to small animals.

Notes: This is the smallest wildcat in North America. The name comes from its short tail, which looks bobbed, or cut short. Look for bobcats near large rocks or other hiding places.

BEAVER

Color: Dark brown.

Size: Body is 3–4 feet (0.9–1.2 m) long. Tail is about 1 foot (0.3 m) long.

Food: Tree bark.

Notes: You may see beavers just before dark or very early in the morning. Look for the V-shaped line of ripples as they swim in ponds and lakes in the forest. The beaver is the largest North American rodent. It is the state animal of New York and Oregon, and the national symbol of Canada.

Reptiles and Amphibians

TIGER SALAMANDER

Color: Dark body with light spots.

Size: 6–13^1/$_2$ inches (15.2–34.3 cm) long.

Food: Earthworms, insects, and small mammals and amphibians.

Notes: After it rains some night, take a flashlight and check near water to see these large salamanders. They live under forest litter and in small animal burrows, especially where the ground is soft enough for them to dig. Tiger salamanders are the largest North American salamanders living on land.

RAT SNAKE

Color: Black is most common. May also have dark stripes or blotches over yellow, brown, or other colors.

Size: 3–8 feet (0.9–2.4 m) long.

Food: Small animals like lizards, mice, and birds.

Notes: This snake is out during the day in spring and fall. Rat snakes can also climb trees and will eat bird eggs from nests. During the hot summer, they are usually out during the cooler hours of night instead of in the daytime.

GARTER SNAKE

Color: Mostly brownish with three narrow, lighter colored stripes, one on top and one on each side.

Size: ^{1}/$_2$–4^1/$_3$ feet (0.2–1.3 cm) long.

Food: Earthworms, frogs, and other amphibians.

Notes: Garter snakes are found in more areas of North America than any other snake. In the forest, look for them near water and other moist areas searching for food.

FROGS

Color: Most are green, brownish, or gray with dark or light stripes and dark blotches or patterns.

Size: Up to 5 inches (12.7 cm) long, depending on the species. Spring peepers are 1 inch (2.5 cm) long.

Food: Insects.

Notes: Frogs are often seen in or near still or slow-moving water.

They are also in moist woodlands and moist forest meadows. Since most frogs are nocturnal, you may hear them before you see them. Spring peepers have a mating call that sounds like a birdsong.

BOX TURTLE

Color: Brownish. May have yellow and orange as well as dark blotches.

Size: 4–8^1/$_2$ inches (10.2–21.6 cm) long.

Food: Earthworms, wild strawberries, mushrooms, and plants.

Notes: These turtles grow to their full size in 20 years, but often live to be 80 years old. Look for them during the day in moist forest areas, especially after it rains. The box turtle is the state reptile of Kansas.

Wildflowers and Fungi

Common blue violet

Canada violet

VIOLETS

Color: Blue, purple, or purplish blue flowers. Others are white and may have yellow on their petals.

Size: Flowers on stems 1–16 inches (2.5–40.6 cm) tall, depending on the species.

Notes: These flowers bloom in the spring through early summer. Look for them coming up through the leaf litter of last fall's fallen leaves. Violets are the state flower of Illinois, New Jersey, and Wisconsin, and the provincial flower of New Brunswick.

Red trillium

Painted trillium

White trillium

TRILLIUM

Color: Flowers are white, pinkish, brownish red, or white with a dark pink center.

Size: 4–20 inches (10.2–50.8 cm) tall. The shortest flowers are in western North America.

Notes: The name *trillium* comes from the three (or "tri") flower petals, three green flower sepals, and three leaves of each plant. The red trillium of eastern North America smells bad, kind of like rotten meat, and attracts flies. Trilliums flower from February to June in western North America and from April to June in eastern North America. This is the provincial flower of Ontario, Canada.

FIREWEED

Color: Pink to purplish flowers.

Size: 2–7 feet (0.6–2.1 m) tall.

Notes: Fireweed is most common along roads and recently burned areas in the summer. This plant is fairly tall and often grows with lots of other fireweed. All that pink is easy to spot. Fireweed is the territorial flower of the Yukon.

COLUMBINE

Color: Reddish orange with yellow centers.

Size: $1/2$–3 feet (0.2–0.9 m) tall.

Notes: Found in moist forest places such as stream edges. The red flowers are usually easy to see, especially on the taller stems. Flowers may appear from April through August.

FUNGI

Color: All colors. Orange, red, yellow, and white are easiest to spot.

Size: Some species of mushrooms and other fungi are several inches tall or wide. Most, however, are much smaller.

Notes: As forest trees die, mushrooms and other fungi may begin to grow on the tree trunks or roots. A lot of fungi are brown and small, blending in on the forest floor among the dead leaves and other forest litter. DO NOT TOUCH mushrooms and other fungi. Many are poisonous and can make you sick.

Amanita mushroom

Sulfur shelf

Shrubs

SUMAC

Color: Leaves are deep green on top, lighter green on bottom. Yellowish green flowers in summer with dark red fruit in the fall. Many sumacs turn orange, bright red, or purplish in the fall.

Size: Up to 30 feet (9.1 m) tall.

Notes: Look for these shrubs along forest edges and other open, sunny areas. Fruit is eaten by many forest birds and small mammals. Groups of sumacs may grow together and form thickets.

WITCH-HAZEL

Color: Yellow flowers, usually in October or November. Dark green leaves turn yellow in fall.

Size: A shrub or small tree 10–25 feet (3.0–7.6 m) tall.

Notes: Found in the eastern United States under deciduous trees and along forest edges and rivers. Witch-hazel is pretty easy to find in late fall when the yellow flowers are out on the leafless branches.

SNOWBERRY

Color: Light pink flowers in early summer. Pea-sized white fruit in late summer and throughout winter. Green leaves.

Size: 3–5 feet (0.9–1.5 m) tall.

Notes: Deer eat the leaves, and birds eat the fruit. Small mammals use snowberry bushes as hiding places. Look along rivers and other places where the ground is moist.

BEARBERRY

Color: Tiny pink flowers in spring. Red fruit in late summer. Dark green leaves.

Size: About 6 inches (15.2 cm) tall.

Notes: This is a very low shrub that spreads across the forest floor. It is called kinnikinnick in western North America. Look for it in open areas, sometimes on sand or near rocks.

Trees (Hardwoods)

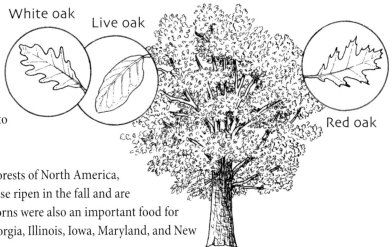

White oak   Live oak   Red oak

OAK

Color: Grayish brown to dark brown bark and grayish green to green leaves.

Size: Usually 20–80 feet (6.1–24.4 m) tall.

Notes: About 60 different kinds of oaks can be found in the forests of North America, mostly south of Canada. All oaks have nuts called acorns. These ripen in the fall and are eaten by squirrels, woodpeckers, deer, and other animals. Acorns were also an important food for Native Americans. Oaks are the state trees of Connecticut, Georgia, Illinois, Iowa, Maryland, and New Jersey, and the provincial tree of Prince Edward Island.

TULIP TREE or YELLOW-POPLAR

Color: Light green leaves, green and light orange tulip-shaped flowers, grayish bark. Leaves turn reddish orange in the fall.

Size: Can be tall, up to 190 feet (57.9 m) high.

Notes: Leaves are oddly shaped and easy to identify. Look for these trees in moist areas of the Eastern and Southeastern Forest regions. Some Native Americans made the trunks into dugout canoes. The tulip tree is the state tree of Indiana, Kentucky, and Tennessee.

BIRCH

Color: White, silvery gray, yellowish, or brown bark, depending on the species. Dark horizontal stripes or blotches are common on the trunks. Leaves are dark green on top, lighter underneath.

Size: One species, called yellow birch, can grow up to 100 feet (30.5 m) tall, but most are 25–80 feet (7.6–24.4 m) tall.

Notes: Look for these trees in moist soil. Strips or pieces of peeled-off bark hang on the trunks of many types of birch trees. Native Americans of northeastern North America used the bark of paper birch trees for the outsides of their canoes. Paper birch is the state tree of New Hampshire. A birch is also the provincial tree of Quebec and Saskatchewan.

MAPLE

Color: Gray, grayish brown, or reddish brown bark, depending on the species. Green leaves. In the fall, leaves of different types of maple turn bright yellow, orange, or bright red.

Size: 30–100 feet (9.1–30.5 m) tall, depending on the species.

Notes: The sap from the sugar maple and black maple in eastern North America is made into maple syrup. Look for maples on hill and mountain slopes, moist areas, and along streams. Maples are the state trees of New York, Rhode Island, Vermont, West Virginia, and Wisconsin.

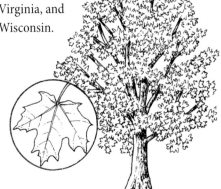

Trees (Conifers)

SPRUCE

Color: Gray, purplish, or reddish brown bark. Dark green leaves are common. Blue spruce leaves are silvery blue.

Size: Most spruce trees are less than 100 feet (30.5 m) tall, although the Sitka spruce in Pacific Northwest forests grows up to 200 feet (61.0 m) tall.

Notes: These trees are found in cool mountain areas and across the boreal forest. Look for their pointed, cone shape near streams and boggy areas. Spruce trees are the state trees of Alaska, Colorado, South Dakota, and Utah, and the provincial trees of Manitoba, Newfoundland, and Nova Scotia.

PINE

Color: Usually brown or grayish brown bark and green leaves.

Size: From the 20-foot (6.1-m) pinyon pine to the almost-200-foot (61.0-m) ponderosa, Jeffrey, and sugar pines.

Notes: There are many kinds of pine trees. All have leaves called needles that are very thin. Most of these needles occur in bunches of two to six and can be several inches (or centimeters) long. Pine trees are found in all North American forests except the lowland tropical rain forest. They are the state trees of Alabama, Arkansas, North Carolina, Idaho, Maine, Minnesota, Nevada, New Mexico, and Montana, and the provincial trees of Alberta and Ontario. The pine's cone and needle cluster is also the state flower of Maine.

DOUGLAS-FIR

Color: Bark is reddish brown on full-grown trees. Leaves are dark yellowish green.

Size: Very tall trees—160–230 feet (48.8–70.1 m) high.

Notes: This is not a true fir tree. Douglas-fir is found at lower elevations in mountain forests than true firs, and its cones hang down, not up. Look under the tree for fallen cones and notice the papery bracts with three prongs sticking out between the scales. This is the state tree of Oregon.

FIR

Color: Gray or reddish brown bark. Leaves can be dark green, bluish green, or dull green, depending on the type of fir.

Size: Most firs grow to at least 100 feet (30.5 m) tall. Balsam fir of northeastern North America grows to 60 feet (18.3 m).

Notes: Fir cones stick up on the branches, unlike most other conifers, whose cones hang down. Deer and grouse eat the leaves, and squirrels eat the seeds. Look for fir trees on the high, steep slopes of mountain forests.

A fir is the provincial tree of New Brunswick, and the territorial tree of the Yukon.

HEMLOCK

Color: All have reddish brown bark and yellowish green to bluish green leaves.

Size: Eastern hemlock is about 75 feet (22.9 m) tall. The mountain hemlock grows to about 95 feet (29.0 m). The western hemlock in the Pacific Northwest is the tallest, at just over 200 feet (61.0 m).

Notes: These trees grow best in protected, cool, moist areas, often in the shade of other trees. Look for the drooping ends of the branches. Eastern hemlocks are eaten by white-tailed deer. A hemlock is the state tree of Pennsylvania and Washington.

Animal Tracks and Signs

The tracks, or footprints, of animals are hard to see on the forest floor because of all the fallen leaves, mosses, and other plants. Your best chance to spot animal tracks is to look on dirt hiking trails, along the muddy or sandy edges of ponds, lakes, and streams, or in the snow during winter.

You can also look for animal signs. A leaf or twig that's been bitten off by deer or elk is an example of an animal sign. And a tree trunk with a scraped area 5 to 6 feet (1.5 to 1.8 m) above the ground may be the sign of black bears living in the area, marking their territory.

Scat, or animal poop, is another type of sign. Deer scat looks like dark seeds or pits from olives. Dried rabbit scat is light brown and the shape and size of large peas. If you look closely, you can see the bits of chopped-up plants the rabbit has eaten. Mouse scat looks like black, lumpy rice.

Animals may be very hard to spot in a forest. But if you know how to identify their tracks and signs, you can figure out which animals live there.

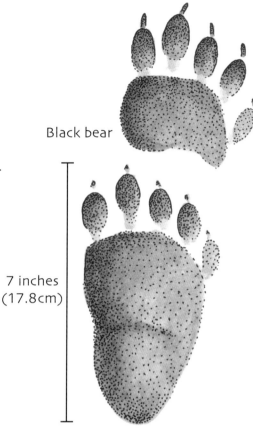

Black bear

7 inches
(17.8cm)

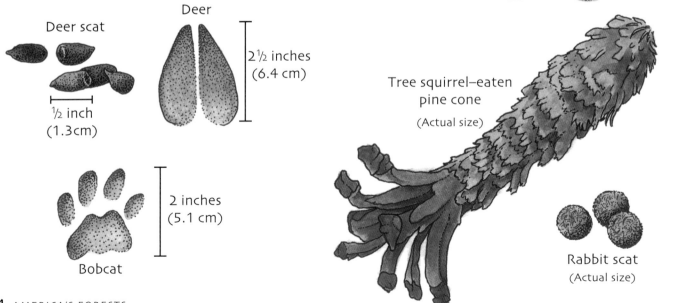

Deer scat

½ inch
(1.3cm)

Deer

2½ inches
(6.4 cm)

Bobcat

2 inches
(5.1 cm)

Tree squirrel–eaten
pine cone

(Actual size)

Rabbit scat

(Actual size)

Glossary

Canopy: The rooflike cover of leaves, branches, and other parts of the tallest trees and plants in the forest.

Climax forest: A forest where succession has stopped and the types of trees remain the same from then on.

Closed forest: A forest where the trees grow really close together and usually shade the forest floor.

Conifer: A tree such as a pine or fir with needlelike leaves and seeds in cones instead of in flowers.

Deciduous: Refers to shrubs and trees that lose their leaves in the fall and grow new ones the next spring.

Evergreen: Refers to shrubs and trees that keep their leaves all year long.

Epiphyte: A plant that grows above the ground on a tree or shrub and gets its water and nutrients from the air in the form of rain, falling leaves, and blowing dust. Also called an air plant.

Forest floor: The lowest part or layer of a forest. This includes the plant litter and earth at the base of most trees and shrubs.

Forest gap: An opening that allows sunlight to reach the forest floor. It is often found in a closed forest and sometimes caused by a large tree falling down.

Hardwood: A word used for broad-leafed trees such as maples and oaks.

Herb layer: The part of the forest beneath the shrubs and short trees where wildflowers, grasses, and ferns grow.

Litter: The dead and fallen leaves, flowers, seeds, fruit, and other plant material lying on the forest floor.

Mast: The acorns, nuts, and other seeds eaten by forest squirrels, birds, and other animals.

Nurse log: A fallen, rotting log usually covered in moss and other small plants where seeds find nutrients and moisture to start growing.

Open forest: A forest whose trees grow far enough apart that sunlight reaches most of the forest floor.

Shrub layer: A middle layer in a forest's understory where shrubs and small trees are found.

Succession: Different types of plants growing in a newly cleared area of forest over a period of time, usually grasses, then shrubs, then trees.

Understory: The shorter plants growing under the canopy of the forest.

Virgin forest: A forest whose trees have never been cut down or burned.

Resources

The places listed below have forest areas open to the public. They may also have hiking trails, a visitor center, and a naturalist or ranger to answer questions. Search for them on the Internet or write to them for more information.

EASTERN FORESTS
Acadia National Park
P.O. Box 177
Bar Harbor, ME 04609-0177

Allegany State Park
New York State Office of Parks
2373 ASP, Route 1, Suite 3
Salamanca, NY 14779-9756

Great Smoky Mountains National Park
107 Park Headquarters Road
Gatlinburg, TN 37738-4102

SOUTHEASTERN FORESTS
Weymouth Woods
Sandhills Nature Preserve
1024 Fort Bragg Road
Southern Pines, NC 28387-7319

WESTERN MOUNTAIN FORESTS
Rocky Mountain National Park
1000 Highway 36
Estes Park, CO 80517-8397

Yosemite National Park
Public Information Office
P.O. Box 577
Yosemite National Park, CA 95389-0577

BOREAL FOREST
Wrangell-St. Elias National Park and Preserve
Mile 106.8 Richardson Highway
P.O. Box 439
Copper Center, AK 99573-0439

Wabakimi Provincial Park
435 James Street South
Suite 221d
Thunder Bay, Ontario
Canada
P7E 6S8

PACIFIC NORTHWEST FORESTS
Redwood National and State Parks
1111 Second Street
Crescent City, CA 95531-4123

Olympic National Park
600 East Park Avenue
Port Angeles, WA 98362-6798

TROPICAL RAIN FORESTS
Corcovado National Park
Osa Peninsula
Puerto Jiménez, Golfito
Costa Rica

Common and Scientific Names

There are two small reddish tree squirrels found in the forests of North America: one is the red squirrel and the other is the Douglas' squirrel. Each of these squirrels is also called a pine squirrel or chickaree. Having more than one common name can be very confusing. But the **scientific name** of an animal or plant is the same all over the world.

Scientific names have two parts. The first part is called the genus and is capitalized. The second part is called the species and is not capitalized. Both parts are underlined or typed in *slanted* letters called italics. If the common name refers to more than one species of the same genus, then the species name is left out and "spp." is written instead.

The following list includes the common names and scientific

Index

Centimeters

Tamiasciurus hudsonicus

Tamiasciurus douglasii